Spider Phobia
Fifteen Minute Therapy

12 techniques that will cure a phobia or fear of spiders in fifteen minutes or less

© James Brackin 2013

All rights reserved. No part of this publication may be reproduced, stored in a retrieval system, or transmitted in any form or by any means electronic, mechanical, photocopying, recording or otherwise without the prior permission of the copyright owner.

This book gives non-specific, general advice and should not be relied on as a substitute for proper medical consultation. The author and publisher cannot accept responsibility for issues, illness or problems arising out of the failure to seek medical advice from a qualified healthcare professional.

Fifteen Minute Therapy.

Finally be rid of your fear of Spiders, with these 12 easy-to use techniques. And do that in seconds or minutes, rather than hours or days because these easy-to-use, practical techniques work very quickly – in fifteen minutes or less.

This is more than just a book as it provides three ways to overcome your phobia:

1. Read the exercises

Every technique in this book is structured in a step-by-step, easy to follow format.

2. Or you prefer listen to the exercises

The icon above shows that this technique is also available as audio file. So you can listen to it on your computer, tablet or smartphone. It's just like having a one-to-one consultancy.

3. Or write down your experiences

This icon in the text it means that your responses could be recorded in the PDF workbook provided. Writing down responses in this way is proven to speed up the healing process.

About the Author.

Based in Sussex, England, Jim Brackin studied motivational and behavioural psychology. Jim is a qualified Master Hypnotherapist (ABH), a Master practitioner of Neuro Linguistic Programming (ANLP, ABNLP), a Master Practitioner of Time Line Therapy (TLTA) and studied Neuro-Associative Conditioning at Mastery University, Hawaii.

The Sky News behavioural expert for three years Jim made regular appearances on the BBC and local radio stations. His opinions and techniques have been featured in national and international newspapers and magazines. In the UK these include The Sun, The Daily Mail, Cosmopolitan and Woman's Own.

What other users say about fifteen minute therapy.

"I am on my 3rd session, it has made me see where the phobia came from and I find the sessions easy to use as they are in small pieces so you don't feel overwhelmed. I am looking forward to getting rid of this phobia and moving on with my life. Each little step doesn't feel like much but I'm hoping to get there in the end. I like that I can do them in my own time when I feel ready with no pressure."

"This is good to make you see all the downsides of holding onto your phobia and what it's holding you back from in your life. It's crazy what it stops you doing and what a hold it has on you. I look forward to not being afraid anymore and moving on with my life."

"Well... I must say I'm very grateful to receive such great relief already from this consultation; your program has been bringing forth many changes in my life so far. It has led me to see that its only useless thought that's hindering my medical visits and injections."

"I have phobia for 27 years since I was 3. Already after the first session I looked at the problem differently. Looking at all the notes I have made the fear now seems unreasonable to me. Injections are still unpleasant to think of but my thinking about it has changed and I will be able to overcome it."

"These are easy exercises to do especially if you listen to them as you can just close your eyes and do each stage without having to stop and read each part."

Contents

An introduction:

Chapter One: Before using fifteen minute therapy.

Chapter Two: Why these fifteen minute therapies work.

Part One: The Detailed Personal History

Chapter Three: How the sessions are structured.

Chapter Four: Finding the phobic trigger.

Chapter Five: Why your phobia has been getting worse.

Chapter Six: Changing the sub-modalities.

Chapter Seven: Removing any secondary gain.

Part Two: The Fifteen Minute Interventions

Chapter Eight: The emotion switch.

Chapter Nine: The music therapy.

Chapter Ten: Word replacement therapy.

Chapter Eleven: Disconnect the connection.

Chapter Twelve: And finally.

An introduction:

The session had just ended. Louise was in shock. It's easy to understand why, an hour and a half earlier she had been living with a lifelong phobia of needles.

"As a little girl I remember lying awake at night, dreading having my rubella jabs. They made us line up in alphabetical order and because my maiden name is Wilkinson, I was right at the back of the queue. By the time they got to me I was hysterical. My husband Dominic enjoys travelling and we both love going on holiday, but have to stick to countries where you don't need jabs. The thought of the needle going into my arm made me sick with fear."

Phobias like this are not uncommon, it's estimated that 20% of adults in the UK suffer from an intense fear or dread, a phobia. Like many other psychological issues they are usually the result of a highly stressful or traumatic event that is linked to something that is present at the time. The trauma of the event and the link to the thing is stored in the unconscious mind. The thing becomes a trigger for the traumatic memory so when you see, think or come into contact with the trigger it brings back the feelings of the traumatic event. The more this happens, the more powerful the trigger and the phobic response become.

It's because of this unconscious connection that most psychological issues it simply cannot be rationalised away, if it could you'd be able to deal with it already. Most phobics know that their fear is irrational, but that doesn't make the fear any less real. Like you, if Louise's phobia could have been easily rationalised away she would have done it many, many years ago.

But now her phobia was finally over. Gone, finished, ended. It simply wasn't there. By removing the link between the traumatic event and the trigger; needles in Louise's case and the traumatic event, thirty years of phobia had simply disappeared in a shade under 90 minutes. Her reaction? "I can't quite believe it, I realised that needles didn't bother me anymore. This year I don't have to worry about where we go on holiday, because having jabs isn't a problem. I can't believe something so simple really works."

The unusual thing about Louise's experience wasn't that she had lost her needle phobia. The process used is something that can be taught to anyone in an afternoon. You'll find many of the basic techniques in this book. The unusual thing about Louise's experience was that it was part of a well-documented Daily Mirror feature on the effectiveness of cognitive psychology. The feature was testing the claims of therapists who use the power of the mind, commonly called 'talking cures' to make lasting change in their clients.

The journalist responsible, Christine Morgan chose Louise because she was a close personal friend. She knew first hand about her phobia and how much it had affected her life. Frankly Christine was doubtful that it was possible to totally remove such a deep-seated fear. This belief had been re-enforced by the reaction of the first therapist to take up the challenge. Initially wanting ten, two-hour CBT sessions the therapist declined the task, walking away after two of the ten sessions because there wasn't enough time. Let's face it, Louise was a hospital pass for any therapist foolish enough to take on the challenge with the certain knowledge that failure would be very publicly reported to millions of Daily Mirror readers. It was potentially a career ending decision.

Christine had heard of work I had done in this area and with a deadline looming, I received an anxious phone call. She asked if I would be prepared to step in at short notice and work with Louise. My decision was instant. I agreed to work with Louise without hesitation, and when I suggested the phobia would be disconnected in one, two-hour session there was a long pause on the other end of the line. During that silence I really expected the phone to go dead. It's not difficult to imagine Christine hanging up, head shaking in disbelief. But like any journalist she instinctively knew that whatever the result it would make a great story.

"Are you serious?"

"Yes."

"Well, if this works you should write a book and share what you do with the rest of us."

It did and this is it. Now I appreciate that on the surface your spider phobia or fear may appear to be quite different to the phobia that Louise suffered from but at a deeper psychological perspective there are many, many similarities. Both are based on an event or events in the past that triggered the symptoms. Both had been getting worse over the years. And both despite your best efforts to rationalise the fear it has refused to go away. Although the event that caused of your problem is different, the structure of your fear and how that fear can be turned down from a psychological perspective, are quite similar.

This is the collection of techniques that I'd use if we were sitting face to face. And if you let me guide you through them you'll have the same result.

Enjoy.

Jim Brackin.

Chapter One: Before using fifteen minute therapy

"Have you ever seen a building being constructed? I not talking about just passing by as construction is happening; I mean watching it evolve over a period of time? If so you may have noticed that once the site is cleared nothing appears to happen for ages. Sure, you be aware that people are working hard; holes are dug, concrete is poured, foundations are laid but despite all that effort to start with there is no noticeable sign of progress.

To the casual observer it could appear that there is a lot of activity with nothing to show for it. Yet we understand that that is not the case. Then everything changes as all of a sudden, as if by magic, the building quickly rises from its foundations and is completed. From the builders perspective however the experience is quite different because they have built buildings before and they know that the most important part of the project is the beginning, the laying of the foundations. It's the part of the building that will never be seen yet they know the quality of the foundations will determine the strength and integrity of the building. They know that laying the foundations for the building is as, if not more, important than the building itself."

Could you imagine if we had access to a first aid kit that would treat our emotional cuts and bruises just as easily as sticking plaster and ointment can our physical ones? Just consider an insecurity aspirin, a sadness plaster or an anxiety bandage. Something that was always there just in case of an emergency.

That's the purpose of this book to provide you with fast and effective sticking plaster for your problem. So that you can, in time of need, pull a technique out of the kit and use it to make an immediate difference. And do that in seconds or minutes rather than hours or days because all the techniques work in less than fifteen minutes, once used a few times some will work instantly.

Then perhaps your experience will be similar to that of someone who has already used these techniques:

"I am currently beset with negative emotions - mainly dread,

frustration, helplessness and rampant anxiety. I have done the technique to change emotions several times this week and found it did make me feel better very quickly and helped me clear my head sufficiently to take some action to help myself.

It really was first-aid."

Soon you'll be able to dip into these techniques to gain control and make quick and lasting changes to your life. In fact you only have to do three things to ensure that you always get a result.

1. Use the techniques only when you are really ready to make a change.

2. Follow the step-by-step instructions.

3. Take all of the credit for the results you get.

Follow these three simple steps and you'll find that all the therapies in your first aid kit work 100% of the time every time without exception. So what do you want to change first?

Knowing when it's time to change

Before using any of the techniques please use this 'Time to change' script or if you prefer let me talk you through it. Wherever you see this icon you can listen to following technique at the url shown.

listen to this therapy:
http://talkingcures.org/spider_phobia/audio

Okay, let's get started. Some people have a reluctance to change that they may not even be aware of and if that's the case this script will flush any issues out into the open so that it can be more easily dealt with. Being aware of any barriers is an essential first step as it will make the process of change quick and easy. To start, ask yourself the following question and listen to your inner voice for a response. It's important at this early stage that you are honest and trust your instincts. Continue to the second question only if the answer is a quick and direct "Yes".

This works best if you read the question out aloud. Start by asking yourself:

1. "Is it okay for me to experience a positive change in the way I feel and have a real experience of the therapy working today?"

An answer will just pop into your head. Make a note of it. If you detect any hesitation in answering the question or your inner voice says something like "I think so", "Probably", "Maybe", "I'll try" or "No" then ask yourself the second question. If you feel a big, fat, instant positive YES then skip the rest of this section.

2. "Is it ok for me to have a positive experience of the techniques working today knowing that I can go back to that old way should I choose?"

Be aware of your reaction. Again only continue if you instinctively feel that the answer is a "Yes". If the answer is still no then move onto question three.

3. "What do I need to know in order for the therapy to benefit me?"

You might be surprised to find that an answer will just pop into your head. When it does ask yourself question four.

4. "Knowing what I now know is it now ok to proceed?"

Listen to your inner voice. If the answer is a Yes continue. If the answer is still no go back and ask question three again.

This sequence of questions ensures that you are really ready to make a change right now. All you have to do is to follow the instructions and remember to take credit for the changes.

What to do if you are not yet ready to change.

Occasionally it's possible that having used the 'Time to change' script you still feel you aren't quite ready. Perhaps you are not sure why. So what does it mean if you keep asking yourself those questions, and you keep getting the answer 'no'?

Well the good news is that the very fact that you are aware of the thing that you want to change in your life means that at some level you are ready to make that change. And that you have the resources already available to do this in a way that is totally safe and beneficial. But sometimes there's a time lag between making a decision and coming to terms with taking action to resolve it, which is simply part of the healing process. It's the effect of the time lag that you are experiencing. There are still a number of choices that you have at this point.

Work on another issue with less emotional intensity.

By working on something else you become used to using the techniques and creating positive change. Pick an issue to work on that has less of an emotional connection as this might well change the way you feel about the bigger issues.

Change the way you feel.

Movement affects our mood and our mood influences our responses. So stop and do something that you really enjoy, something that makes you feel good about yourself or something that increases your energy level. Take a walk, have a bath, read a book, play some music, talk to a friend, watch a comedy programme. It really doesn't matter as long as it works for you. Then when you feel different, use the 'Time to change' script again, you'll be surprised at the difference.

Ask yourself these questions.

It's possible that on some level you are not totally comfortable with the effects of the change. To reassure yourself that any changes made will be safe and beneficial ask either of these questions. "Knowing that any new insights can only help me, it's ok for me to safely change how I feel isn't it?" "What else would I need to know in order to proceed?"

Give it time.

Time is a great healer, so come back to this particular issue at a later date. You might be surprised to find that you'll feel differently about it later. Just leaving it a few minutes, hours or days could make all the difference because maybe you haven't yet got the one distinction on the issue that you need to proceed.

Fifteen minutes to change emotions

Life is full of experiences, not all of which are pleasant. Sometimes the emotions attached to our life experiences, especially the negative ones, can surface in our minds like unwanted guests who refuse to leave. Resulting in us dwelling on these memories that crowd out the many positive memories we all have.

Whilst sometimes it may be appropriate to feel these emotions wouldn't it be great if you could just turn down the intensity so they are less painful? Imagine if you could turn them off so that you felt better now than you did previously. Then you could just put them behind you and get on with your life. That is exactly what this technique is designed to do.

listen to this therapy:
http://talkingcures.org/spider_phobia/audio

Pick a memory that has a negative feeling or emotion attached to it. If this is the first time you have used this technique pick something that was not a major event. Take a few small steps before you start to run. Preferably choose a memory with a feeling that you would like to reduce or eliminate. We all imagine things in different ways, some people see a picture, others get a feeling of the event, just trust that it's there so however you imagine this memory the process will work for you.

Now get in touch with that memory and all of the associated emotions. To do this;

Remember the event.

See what you saw.

Hear what you heard.

Know what you knew.

Feel what you felt.

You'll notice that as you do this the memory becomes more intense, clear and emotive. Keeping it firmly in mind, answer these questions, follow the instructions and notice how the feelings and emotions you had for the memory start to change.

Is the memory in colour or black and white?

If it's in colour make the image in your head black and white.

If it's already in black and white turn the contrast down and

make the picture dull. If it helps, imagine reaching for and

turning the contrast dial until the picture is really dull.

Is the memory a movie or still frame?

If it's a movie make it still.

If it's a still frame turn the image upside-down.

Do you see the memory through your own eyes or as if you are watching it on a TV. screen?

If it's through your own eyes imagine watching it on a small

TV screen.

If the image is already on a TV screen imagine the screen

shrinking to the size of a postage stamp.

Are there any sounds associated with the memory?

If so turn the volume down until you cannot hear them.

Are there any feelings associated with the memory?

If so imagine they are pulled away from you, and sucked

back into the memory.

Keeping the image exactly how it is now notice that the emotions associated with the event have dramatically reduced or even totally disappeared. Have they just reduced or are they totally gone now? Either way, congratulations. The change emotions technique has had an effect. Finally, to make the effect permanent imagine the screen flashing on and off three times before fading back into your memory.

How this works.

This Fifteen Minute Therapy is effective because it changes the sensory based information that the brain uses at an unconscious level to encode meaning to our memories. It is this sensory-based information that tells us what the memory means and triggers the emotions that you feel. Although we all encode our memories slightly differently, hence the different options in the script, there are certain commonalities that are shared by all of us. So by changing the sensory code what you were actually doing was changing the meaning of the memory at an unconscious level. That's why the emotions change so quickly and why the process doesn't need to make any logical sense. Use this technique on any feelings or emotions that you wish to reduce in intensity.

Congratulations, you have taken the first step towards becoming your own fifteen-minute therapist.

Chapter Two: Why these fifteen minute therapies work

Externally the internet, social media and television exert a powerful influence. Over time their continuous stream of information informs opinion, changes behaviour and provides a window on the outside world that has a direct effect on our thoughts, feelings, emotions and attitudes. Internally your thoughts have exactly the same effect on your body. Your thoughts are the body's live 24-hour news reports, the tweet that's trending worldwide and is broadcast directly into the living rooms of each of the 100 trillion cells in your body. With one small but important difference. You have totally control over the things you choose to think.

The neurotransmitters that pass information around your brain can be found in every part of your body. This means that every organ, every muscle, every cell is listening to your thoughts. Consciously you have already decided what is important, what to believe so at this unconscious level everything you say or think about yourself is taken as an absolute truth. Every cell will be affected and directed by your truth, whatever you decide that truth is.

Once a 'new age' concept, there is now scientific evidence that your thoughts directly determine the quality of your life. If you are happy, sad, in love, lonely, excited, bored, fulfilled, frustrated, expectant, worried, calm or stressed it's all a result of your thoughts. But the science takes it even further as demonstrates that our physical wellbeing is also affected by what we think.

A story from Great Ormond Street

In the early 1990's when fundraising for Great Ormond Street Children's Hospital I came across a remarkable story. A young boy diagnosed with leukaemia was being treated with chemotherapy. In addition to this treatment he was encouraged to use visualisation techniques to aid his treatment.

His imagination was set to work and he visualised his white blood cells as strong and powerful white knights charging around his system killing off those nasty 'black knight' leukaemia cells.

He went into remission much faster than would normally be expected. Although this could have been a coincidence he believed that "…the knight medicine was already making him better."

This little boy was not the only one to use visualisation and not the only one who seemed to progress much faster than those who did not. Now, encouraging children to use visualisation techniques is much more commonplace than it was then.

A study from America

Stanford psychiatrist David Spiegel originally conducted a medical study to set out to prove that the mental state of patients did not influence their ability to survive cancer.

He chose eighty-six women with breast cancer that had advanced beyond the help of conventional treatment. Forty-three of the group were given a combination of weekly psychotherapy and lessons in self-hypnosis. During the weekly sessions he encouraged them to change the way they thought about their cancer and to use the hypnosis to strengthen their immune systems.

Spiegel followed the progress of the group for ten years. He was amazed to find that the forty-three women who received psychotherapy and hypnosis survived on average twice as long as those that did not. Ten years after the original study all of the women that were still alive were from the therapy group.

So the study that set out to prove that the mental state of patients did not influence their ability to survive cancer actually proved exactly the opposite.

It's all in the mind

The placebo effect is well known. It is a measured, observed, or felt improvement in health and well being that is not directly attributable to an active element in the treatment. Even though the placebo effect is 'all in the mind' it can exert a powerful effect on the body. So much so that psychologist Irving Kirsch believes that the effectiveness of Prozac and similar drugs may be attributed almost entirely to the placebo effect. "The critical factor is our beliefs about what's going to happen to us. You don't have to rely on drugs to see profound transformation."

So having a positive attitude may be directly related not only to physical well being but also speed of recovery from injury or illness. Objective measurements of symptoms such as blood pressure and post-operative swelling have found real physical changes can and do.

A report for the House of Lords Science and Technology Committee in 2000 reported 'The placebo effect is not just an imagined experience but can positively improve objective biological measures of health.' and that 'Evidence from a wide range of studies indicates that placebo therapies in the context of conventional medicine can provide some relief from a huge range of conditions including allergies, angina, some forms of cancer, cerebral infarction, depression, diabetes, epilepsy, multiple sclerosis, ulcers and warts.' The report then suggests that 'Part of the conventional doctor's armoury may include inert capsules and sugar pills.' And that 'All treatments, physically active or otherwise, have a psychological impact…' and should be considered '…an essential part of any holistic therapy.'

In the same report Professor Patrick Bateson, Vice President of the Royal Society explained how your thoughts affect you physically '…when somebody suffers chronic stress, bereavement or loses a job, under those conditions they are much more prone to disease and more likely to get cancer, and now it is believed that this is because of suppression of the immune system … so if you do the opposite of that and give the patient some reassurance and if they are given a treatment which they believe in, then this will enhance the immune response.'

In 2013 research by Herbert Benson of the Massachusetts General Hospital in Boston discovered that meditation can boost the activity of genes that improve immune system. It's already known that 'short periods of stress have psychological effects that are harmful in the long term' but it now appears that the opposite is also true. In his study a test group who meditated for just as a few minutes a day saw a measurable improvement in cellular energy, an increase insulin production and reduction of the wearing and aging process of cells. Also the genes that controlled chronic inflammation became less active which reduced the chance of high blood pressure and heart disease. Blood samples taken from the test subjects showed that these gene changes happened within minutes and that regular meditation makes these beneficial changes long-term. He is now looking at using meditation to help high blood pressure, inflammatory bowel disease and cancer.

Fifteen Minutes for Life

The Fifteen Minute Therapy for Life is designed to increase the amount of positive thoughts you have and reduce the number of negative thoughts. If you agree with the work of David Spiegel, Professor Bateson or Herbert Benson, this will not only make you feel a whole lot better it should also enhance the immune system.

When working with a client for the first time I often use this simple therapy to flush out the triggers for unwanted habits. Try it for yourself and experience how your thoughts directly influence how you feel.

Although it's effective to do this exercise in your head, it will not have the same impact as physically writing it down on paper. So, for maximum impact before you start find a pen and actively participate. If you would like me to talk you through this therapy, you'll find an audio version of this therapy at:

listen to this therapy:
http://talkingcures.org/spider_phobia/audio

Step One. To start score on a scale of 1 (low, unhappy, depressed) to 10 (high, joyful, ecstatic), how you feel right now. Go with the first number that pops into your head.

Score 1-2-3-4-5-6-7-8-9-10

Step Two. Now think of three events that have happened in your life that were unpleasant or distressing. You know the ones I mean, those events that when you think of them, you feel sad or upset. Write a sentence as to why they affected you and how you felt at the time. It's important that you only write one sentence.

Wherever there is an open question you'll notice grey text in italic directly underneath. It is provided as example of the type of answers you could give for each question. The text is not intended to direct your own answers. Although it's possible they may be similar.

Event One:

The death of my mother. I felt alone, bereft and afraid without her.

Event Two:

Being bullied at school, specifically the fear of leaving the protection of the school gates and running the gauntlet to get home.

Event Three:

Being rejected by a prospective employer, and being made to feel worthless like I was six inches tall.

Step Three. With those events in mind score on a scale of 1-10 how do you feel now?

Score 1-2-3-4-5-6-7-8-9-10

Step Four. Now sit up straight and look up towards the ceiling. It's very important to change your body posture at this point. So take a couple of seconds to shuffle around on your seat, sit up straight, put your shoulders back and look up.

Only when you have done that remember those events that are well and truly behind you. Now it's possible, on reflection, that something positive may have come out of those events. If so write them down, capture what they are.

If anything good came out of Event One it was:

I realised that the love we have for each other is timeless and that she is always with me. Nothing can change that.

In hindsight a positive from Event Two could have been:

Those bullies made me stronger. I had to stand on my own two feet, and because of that I have always been able to do so.

Perhaps a beneficial thing to come from Event Three was:

I was so lucky not to get that job. Imaging working for someone who enjoyed making others feel small. Two months later I got the job of my dreams.

If nothing comes to mind that's ok simply move on.

Step Five. This is the fun bit. Write down the five best things that have happened so far in your life. Write at least two sentences on each, why they were great, how they affected you, how they made you feel and the effect they had on you.

Event One

Meeting Jane. I feel so lucky that I was ready to be with my soulmate. We share so many wonderful times together.

Event Two

Watching the sunset from the balcony of the Hilton Waikoloa in Hawaii. What a beautiful place, what a wonderful three weeks.

Event Three

Watching James, my son, score two goals in his first match for the senior football team. What a proud moment that was.

Event Four

Winning the artist of the year award a school. Having to go up to receive it in front of everyone was scary yet thrilling and emotional.

Event Five

Realising that I was comfortable with who I am. Knowing that my opinion is as useful, important and as valid as anyone else's.

Step Six. With the five best things in mind score on a scale of 1-10 how you feel now?

Score 1-2-3-4-5-6-7-8-9-10

So how do you feel right now?

Good?

Better than before?

Typically, when my clients use this therapy, they start with a score which then gets lower when they think about the unpleasant events in their lives. When they begin to remember all of the positive events that have happened to them their score gets higher. They may also realise that what were unpleasant events did in fact, in hindsight, have something positive hidden inside them. Is this what you have just experienced?

When it's pointed out that the only thing that has really changed is what they chose to think about. That it's the same life and the same memories and that the only difference was the focus of their attention. And it was this that made the difference in the score. At that point they realise that they have some control over how they feel.

To feel bad is easy just choose to dwell on the negatives in life. Pretty quickly feelings of despondency, sadness and depression will follow. Or choose to remember the good times and feelings of happiness, joy, contentment, peace and fulfilment come just as easily.

But with this understanding comes a responsibility and it's not an easy one for many people to accept. That's because there is only one person who can choose what you think about.

You. You alone.

Here is some really good news. And a very, very important point for you to remember is that YOU HAVE TOTAL CONTROL OVER WHAT YOU CHOOSE TO THINK ABOUT. Your thoughts are your choice, your creation, your responsibility.

If your thoughts really do determine the quality of your life, and to help you have more positive thoughts and less negative thoughts we have to ask the following question. What is it that determines the quality of your thoughts?

Fifteen minutes to eliminate your killer questions

In order to make sense of the world around us we all constantly evaluate situations by using an internal dialogue (some might call it self-talk) that consists of a string of questions. This question asking process is hardwired into each and every one of us. In fact it's one of the things that makes humans different to other animals. At an unconscious level we continually ask questions like:

"What does this mean?"

"How will it affect me?"

"What should I do?"

Whenever your self-talk, your internal dialogue asks a question, your unconscious mind is programmed to give you an answer. And we are asking questions all of the time. So in every situation your thoughts, even if our conscious mind is unaware of it, are determined by the questions we ask, and as we have already discovered, your thoughts determine the quality of your experience.

I find that clients who have a psychological or physiological issue tend to use a different internal dialogue, a different set of questions, to people who do not. They ask different questions and because of this they get different answers. For example someone who's depressed might ask "Why do bad things always happen to me?" "Will that make me worse?" "Why am I powerless to prevent it?" And guess what, if you ask negative questions you'll get negative answers. This becomes an ongoing process, a habit, a downward spiral.

The questions you ask and the answers you get actually determine the meaning of the event for you. For example, you have probably noticed that an event that would devastate one person will hardly matter to another. It's all a question of perception.

This technique is designed to help you flush out all of those 'killer negative questions' or their answers that you use on a regular basis. It's a simple three step process. Use it for a week, and I guarantee that you will see a noticeable improvement in your quality of life.

Step 1. Write them down. This targets your questions for removal.

Step 2. Scramble them up. This breaks the habit of using them.

Step 3. Replace them with something better.

Step 1. Write down your five 'killer questions'.

These will be questions you use on a regular basis, perhaps without realising it. These are the questions that don't serve you. The questions you use to beat yourself up. The questions that are about to become a thing of the past. They will be negative; Why can't I?…, What stops me?…, Why don't I ever?. You get the idea. Now write down you own killer questions now.

* You'll get the most benefit from this exercise if you are completely honest with yourself. You know what your questions are alternatively you could write down the answers you get instead. You'll know them as the phrases you say to yourself on a regular basis when something goes wrong. The phrases you use to beat yourself up.

If you think you don't know them remember a recent negative situation, one where you were down on yourself and notice that they come to mind as soon as you start to write. So start writing now.

Situation 1.

Why do I always mess things up?

Situation 2.

Why am I so stupid?

Situation 3.

Why do bad things always happen to me?

Situation 4.

What stops me finding true love?

Situation 5.

Why don't I ever listen to good advice?

Step 2. Scramble the old.

When seen on paper some of the questions might seem rather harsh now. That's okay. Better to have them out in the open. Now you can see them for what they really are and start to mess with them. The most effective way to scramble a question is to change how it feels, change how it sounds and then change the content.

To change the feeling, change your body language. My preferred method to do this is to stand up. Then stand on one leg and whilst hopping around keeping your balance say your question. For example if your question was "Why do I always mess things up?"

say a word each time you hop. Many people find it hard to do this without laughing out loud.

To change the sound, change the voice in your head. Imagine how "Why do I always mess things up?" would sound in a high-pitched squeaky voice. Change your tone and the pitch of your voice and read out your question. Notice how your feelings change.

To change the content, speak the question out loud but backwards. For example if one of your questions was "Why do I always mess things up?" then you say "Up things mess always I do why?" So remembering the last time you used this question, get a picture of that time, connect with the feelings and read it out backwards now. Notice how silly it sounds, how ridiculous it feels. Repeat this three times.

Step 3. Replace with the new.

Now we are going to add the new questions that will better serve you and start to change your perceptions. These questions will move you forward, towards a brighter future. They will be stated in the positive. For example, "How can I learn from ….?", "What's the good in …?", "What's wonderful about …?" Choose those that inspire you. Now write down the life changing questions that are relevant to you.

Your five life changing questions

Change Question 1.

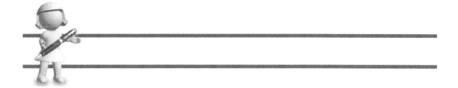

How can I learn from facing up to a family bereavement?

Change Question 2.

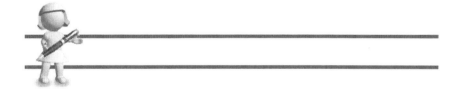

What's the good in being made to run the gauntlet?

Change Question 3.

What's wonderful about coming face-to-face with a bigot?

Change Question 4.

If there was one positive in all of this, what would it be?

Change Question 5.

Will this matter at all in five years time?

Imagine a situation where in the past you would have used an old killer question and replace it with one of your new empowering questions. Imagine the difference the new question makes to the way you feel.

Now imagine a time in the future, which had it have happened before you may have used that old killer question. Replace it with one of your new empowering questions. Notice the difference it makes.

Read through each one of your life changing questions, review them daily for the next seven days and you'll find that they become the questions you ask by habit. By using this process you have taken a major step forward because over the coming weeks you will become aware of the dramatic difference these questions have made to the quality of your life.

Chapter Three: How the sessions are structured

Now we have done the groundwork let me tell you how the rest of this therapy is structured. There are two parts to this phobia cure, In the first four sessions we'll conduct a detailed personal history that maps out the causes, triggers and feelings you associate with spiders. All you need to do is read or listen to the session - much like you would if you were a client attending a one-to-one therapy session. These sessions lay the foundations for effectively removing the phobia. However tempting it might be, it's important that you complete the detailed personal history section before jumping into the interventions.

Then, you'll be ready for the remaining intervention sessions where I'll set about guiding you through a series of practical, effective treatments that are proven to reduce, or totally remove your old spider fears for good. Although it's hard to predict at this stage which one of these interventions will work for you - I do know that one or a combination of them will.

You can expect to see a real change in your fear when you start on these 'intervention' sessions. Also a number of these sessions are specifically designed to help you notice the changes you have already made during the process, so you can be aware of exactly the difference that these spider phobia treatments will make.

Chapter Four: Finding the phobic trigger

The first step to removing your spider phobia is to recall what caused it in the first place. To begin we'll need a better understanding the 'significant emotional event' that originally triggered this phobia. This is the first step on the path to removing your fear of spiders, it'll take around ten minutes and you'll need a pen and paper or some way to record what happens. These first few sessions will lay out the foundations for the interventions to follow. They are very similar to the detailed personal history that I would undertake if we were doing this face to face. Because of that these first sessions are very important as they will make the changes we make later much more effective and long-lasting.

Most clients find it easier if they let me talk them through the process whilst they make notes and concentrate on the session. If you would prefer that, then use the audio link and let me guide you through the process.

The first thing we have to do is to associate you with that old fear of spiders.

This is an important step as without this connection the interventions will not be effective, so take some time over it. I'd like you to think about something that will help to 'loosen up' the phobia. Logically, there would have been a time in your life, a first time that spiders ever became a problem. Before that time in the past you were ok, then this time, this event in your life happened and since then the fear of spiders has been around.

Your spider phobia can be traced back to a 'Significant Emotional Event' which was the very first time that you linked the event, in which spiders featured, to the negative emotions you now feel.

From that point on the spider becomes a trigger, a catalyst for the emotion because it is associated and neurologically linked or 'anchored' to the emotion. Which is why, every time you think of or see a spider, the emotion - usually fear comes flooding back. Over time this happens so often that you are not actually reacting to the situation itself, but the negative emotions you have built up since that first significant emotional event.

From a therapy perspective your phobia is the anchoring process being attached to an inappropriate emotion. This is not uncommon as the anchoring process is something that we naturally use to remember important events. For example, you could hear a piece of music and instantly be transported back to a time, place or event in your life that was significant. This is a positive anchor at work, and we all have thousands of them stored in our memory.

A phobia is an extreme version of a psychological anchor which is linked to a negative emotion.

Because they can be so useful anchors are easy to create. In a well quoted experiment, Martin Seligman an American psychologist associated a small electric shock to subjects who looked at certain images. Only two to four shocks were enough to create a negative anchor or phobia to images of spiders or snakes, while a much larger number of shocks were needed to cause a neurological link to images of flowers. The key factors are the intensity of the experience, in this instance the pain of the shock and the number of repetitions needed to create the link.

In real life rather than in laboratory conditions it is much easier to create a phobia in just one significant emotional event. That's because your brain learns very quickly in emotionally intense situations - you only have to touch a naked flame once to realise that it's not something you wish to repeat.

listen to this therapy:
http://talkingcures.org/spider_phobia/audio

The purpose of this first part of the process is to identify the significant emotional event.

If you could think back, you could remember that time because for the phobia to form the event that triggered it will be stored in your memory. Even if you don't remember the exact details you'll be able to access the feelings, emotions or get a sense of that event - and that's enough for this process to work. Just go with your first impressions of that first time that you can remember having a fear of spiders. In a moment I'm going to ask you a question and you should answer it with the first thing that pops into your head.

But first, let me explain how these details, feeling, emotions and impressions should 'pop' into your head by asking you a few other questions;

"What colour is your front door?"

"When did you last see the sun set?"

"Do you like the taste of dark chocolate?"

The answers to those three questions just popped into you head - perhaps with an impression of the front door, an image of the sun set and the taste of chocolate.

Before I asked those three questions you weren't thinking of the front door, the sun or dark chocolate - they just surfaced from your memory. That's exactly how you should answer the question I'm about to ask, let it surface from your memory.

Now the question and remember go with the first answer that pops up.

"If you were to know, the time in your life when you had the very first fear of spiders, the memory of which triggered all future fears, how old were you?"

Make a note of your answer.

Now, think back to that earliest memory. Remember what you can and squeeze back into that younger body and remember that first memory of being upset by that encounter with a spider.

Remember all that you can about it and write it down. Pay particular attention to what you saw, what was said, how you felt and what you experienced. If you start writing the first thing that comes into your head, more and more details, impressions, feelings and emotions will begin to surface so capture them all.

Typically this first event has very little emotion or fear attached to it and I'll explain why in the next session, however if, for any reason, the memories are distressing or uncomfortable then stop.

Stop and imagine you are sitting comfortably and watching that old memory play out on one of those small old black and white 1960's television sets. See the memory projected onto that old black and white screen and the feelings and emotions surrounding the memory will then quickly disappear and you can continue to write down what you remember. In fact if you do this you may actually remember more about that first event. Whatever you remember write it down.

Once you have finished, writing everything down that is, you may want to look back at what you have written. Often seeing the old memory laid bare on paper in this way begins to loosen the grip of the old fear as you can re-evaluate that first experience from the perspective of who you are now, knowing what you know now.

Look at what you have written, it may already have begun to make you feel differently now, to remove some of that old fear you used to feel about spiders.

I'll write again next week with another part of the detailed personal history process you can use to finally be rid of this old problem.

Chapter Five: Why your phobia has been getting worse

Do you want to know why your Spider Phobia has been getting worse instead of better? From a therapy perspective the way that all phobias develop is virtually identical, in every instance, no matter what the actual phobia is or who develops it. In some ways this is a big advantage for us because I can help you tackle your phobia knowing that the sequence of interventions we use to reduce or stop it are proven to work.

Many of the common elements of how a spider phobia starts and subsequently develops are rooted in a past experience, as we experienced from the previous session.

All phobias develop as a result of a significant emotional event that links in this instance spiders to your phobic reaction. If you remember back to your own experience, you reacted to what was happening at the time, and that event was the first time that you had associated spiders with a negative emotion. Now obviously I don't know exactly what you wrote in the last session but it's very likely that the first time you had a bad experience with spiders the emotion you felt wasn't the fear you have now - well at least not in the way you experience right now.

That's another common element to the way that phobias develop, the emotions you feel now are much stronger than they were that first time. You are not alone, it's the same for everyone - that the way you feel has been building over the years. When you look back you could probably measure how your reaction has become more and more intense. But don't do so just yet as that's what we will be doing in a few minutes.

One of the reasons that your spider phobia is getting worse and not better is because of something called a gestalt.

A gestalt is the sum total of all the spider related feelings you have ever had - both good and bad. Think of the feelings you experience each time as the individual bricks in a brick wall, on their own they could be dealt with, but when cemented together they form a strong barrier. And for you most if not all of the experiences have been bad, perhaps very bad. And every time you have another bad experience another brick is placed into the wall and over time it gets higher and higher, stronger and stronger. It builds on each 'event' triggering and adding to your fear. Each time stronger and stronger till you get to a tipping point, a point where what might have been a controllable anxiety becomes a fear and the fear develops into a phobia. Left unchecked, you don't even need a physical event to trigger the fear - it might be that you have got to the stage where just seeing or talking about a spideris enough to prompt a reaction.

That's how a fear becomes a phobia

Once you reach this point you are not really reacting to an event - you are reacting to the gestalt - the sum of all the bad feelings you have accumulated over the years. Actually whenever someone's reaction is out of all proportion to an event, that is why. They are not reacting to the actual event, they are reacting to the gestalt - they are reacting to the sum total of their previous experience.

That's why the next part of this process is to start to remove the cement that holds the bricks in that gestalt wall together. As like any wall, without the cement that binds it together, it is much easier to pull down.

If you could plot the development of your phobia from the past, to the present and into the future, you'll know that like all things it had a beginning it has a present and therefore it must have an end. Born at that first event the negative emotion has, over time, grown to what it is now and during that development it had grown even stronger.

The first part of removing gestalt, so that you can finally reduce the effect of this fear of spiders, is to identify some of the words that you have used to describe how it has made you feel at different times.

So let's begin.

If you could use just four words to describe the feelings you have had regarding spiders write them down.

Now, look at what you have written and think about the feeling that is behind all of those feelings, that deeper feeling that you must feel in order to for those four to exist. Looking at the four words ask yourself this question.

Which of these four words is the one that makes the other three happen?

For example if you had written the words 'worry', 'fear', 'pain' and 'dread', in order for all of those feelings to exist you may well feel that the underlying emotion or main emotion you have is 'fear'. There will be one of those words which is most emotive, it is the core emotion that drives all of them. The important thing is to reduce your spider phobia down to one core, or base emotion.

You'll know when you have the core emotion when you know it's the underlying feeling that if taken away all the others would disappear. You'll know if you have successfully found the core emotion, it is the foundation that if removed would make the whole brick wall come crashing down. When you have it, check by asking yourself this question.

If I could magically remove the feeling of [insert your core emotion] when around spiders, would my response to spiders disappear or be reduced?

As before go with the first answer that pops into your head. If you are not sure or get a 'no' simply go back and repeat the process. But if you can answer with an instinctive 'yes', then we can move onto working on the other reason why this old phobia has been a problem for so long and then we can get on with the business of finally pushing that wall down once and for all.

Chapter Six: Changing the sub-modalities

In this session we'll find out exactly how 'phobic' you are to spiders. There are some phobias that seem to have no sense, no purpose, no rhyme or reason but some have their origins rooted in a basic survival instinct. And because you had a bad experience in the past I would suggest that spiders could fall into that category. It is a perfectly natural thing, a part of your defence mechanism that we will make less sensitive during this process.

Before we start, let me totally clear about what this process will do. It will stop you reacting to the gestalt - the core emotion you uncovered in the previous session - which sums up all your previous experiences of spiders. Think of it as resetting your emotional response back to neutral, how it was before the phobia started.

Instead of that heightened or intense reaction to spiders, you'll be able to react to each situation on its own merits. The vast majority of the time you'll feel none of those previous emotions because they will be firmly behind you. Resetting your emotional response means in some instances you feel wary or uneasy, because that response may be a perfectly rational and reasonable reaction based on the circumstances in which you find yourself.

In essence the purpose of this session of the Spider Phobia treatment is to measure your existing emotional reaction so that you can accurately measure how much it reduces during this process.

Subjective Units of Distress.

We do this by using a well proven method call Subjective Units of Distress or SUDS. SUDS is a scale of 0 to 10 for measuring the subjective intensity of disturbance or distress experienced by someone in a particular context. You self-access where you are on the scale of 0 to 10.

A score of 0 would mean normal, relaxed, no reaction right through to 10 which would be panic, stressed, uncontrollable fear. In this way we can use the SUDS as a benchmark to evaluate your progress through this process. And might I suggest that when you get your score down to a three or less the old spider phobia will be well and truly gone. From experience I know one of the sessions will have a dramatic effect on your SUDS score.

The thing I can't predict is that exactly where in the process that will happen. It could be right now, using the technique below, it could be after we have gone through most of the interventions. I simply don't know.

I guess that's the real benefit of doing this one-to-one, is that I would have an instinct of which intervention to use first and know the effect it has. In this instance you'll have to decide when it's reduced or disappeared totally. And that's where SUDS comes in, it is the one technique I can give you that can be used to make a measured decision, in exactly the same way that I would if we were sitting together in the same room.

Remember that SUDS stands for subjective units of distress - and there is a clue in the title as to how it should be used. In order to use SUDS effectively you will need to remember the time when you were most scared of spiders, the time when you felt the fear the most. Now you will only have to do this for a few moments but it is important that you feel the fear, if only to measure how much it changes. This is the only part of this process that is uncomfortable, and it will only last for a few moments. During this process, some people notice a really big change and others notice a smaller change. Both are good, as the important thing is that you go through the steps and begin to notice how you begin to feel differently about that old spider phobia.

 listen to this therapy:
http://talkingcures.org/spider_phobia/audio

The SUDS technique

Step One - Remember the first event

Firstly, remember that time in the past that you felt the most fear of spiders and see what you saw, hear what you heard, feel what you felt and know what you knew at that time. Picture it in your mind to the point where the emotions start to rise when you feel the emotions at their height pinch the little finger of your left hand against your left thumb. Do this for fifteen seconds or until your old spider fear is at its peak.

Step Two - Score how you feel

Next score how you feel on the SUDS scale of one to ten. Ten being uncontrollable fear and zero being totally relaxed. Make a note of the number you come up with.

Score 1-2-3-4-5-6-7-8-9-10

Step Three - Change your state

Now let go of that old memory. To do this, change your state. So if you are sitting down stand up, if you are standing up sit down. Shake your hands, imagine they have water on them and you are trying to shake it off. It might seem strange but trust me, this stage is very important as it changes your neurological state and makes the spider memory recede into the background. Do this for thirty seconds or until the feeling disappears.

Phew! Ok that's good, we are halfway there.

What you have actually done by following this process is set up two different neurological states; one for the phobia state and one for your relaxed state. In a moment we'll disrupt the phobia state. This works in much the same way as a TENS machine. TENS or transcutaneous electrical nerve stimulation is a highly effective, non-invasive way to reduce the effect of pain. This works by sending an electrical impulse along the nerves which has the effect of blocking and confusing other impulses trying to reach the brain. As a result the pain is dramatically reduced and it's the same techniques that we are about to use.

Step Four - disrupting the phobia

What I'd like you to do next is to revisit that 'phobia' state. So sit back down if you were standing up and pinch your left thumb and little finger together. The fear of spiders should to some degree return. Think about that old memory, your fear of spiders. Whist feeling those old fearful feelings, stand up and start shaking the water off your hands. Try to hold onto those of feelings of fear and still shake those hands. You may find, to your surprise that they have less of a hold on you. That they simply start to ebb away and if they do, ebb away that is, simply let them go. Continue to shake for another thirty seconds, just for the sheer fun of it. And remember, no smiling now as this is meant to be serious stuff! Ok you can stop shaking your hands now.

Step Five - new feelings, new emotions

Now, try to get back that old fear, the one that you scored earlier. See what you saw, hear what you heard, feel what you felt and know what you knew at that time. Picture it in your mind. Then just start to shake your hands while remembering that old memory. As you do this, score how you now feel on the SUDS scale of one to ten. Ten being uncontrollable fear and zero being totally relaxed. Make a note of the new SUDS score you come up with.

Score 1-2-3-4-5-6-7-8-9-10

Step Six - Calibrate the difference.

Is your second SUDS number lower than the earlier number? If so congratulations! You have made a big positive step to finally putting that old spider thing behind you once and for all. As long as you noticed a difference we are moving in the right direction. Also make a quick mental note of how you feel differently. Now I accept that you probably can't be waving your hands around the next time you find yourself in that old situation, although it would make the anxiety disappear, so I'll share with you some more interventions that will consolidate the first steps we have taken today.

Now let's begin to change some memories.

Everyone knows that we take in information from the outside world using our five senses of touch, vision, sound, taste and smell. But what many people don't realise is that we also use those same five senses to internalise or process that outside information. If you think about any memory that you have what you recall about it are the sounds, sights, sensations, smells and tastes you experienced at that time.

Try it, think about any memory that you have, in fact pick one right now. Choose a happy memory, one that brings a smile to your face as you remember it and as you do, remember it that is, keep in mind that you will be remembering pictures, hearing the sounds associated with it, feeling what you felt. Depending on the memory it may even evoke certain tastes and smells.

Any memory that you have will be remembered in the same way, using a combination of those five senses. Typically we all have one of our senses that is dominant over the others, it's the one that we are most comfortable with. If you listen carefully to the language people use, it becomes easy to understand which of their senses is most dominant. People use verbs, adverbs and adjectives which are mainly sensory based words when they talk, and they will tend to use one type of sensory group more than another. This is a clue to their dominant sense.

You hear these clues all the time, you see then on the T.V. you might even feel them during a heated discussion. People say things like, "*That rings a bell*", "*I can see what you are saying*". "*How do you feel*?" All of these are little clues as to the senses people use internally to represent their memories. So, how is knowing this going to help make your spider phobia a thing of the past? I said earlier that we use these sensory based words to describe our memories. In fact the words we use to describe something actually help to define the experience we have of it.

Put simply if we change the way we describe something we are actually re-writing our experience or memory of that thing. And by doing that we change the memory we have of it. Remember the work we did previously on the gestalt of your phobia, it was the thing that was making the phobia stronger over time? Well this is the how that process worked; the gestalt was driven by the sensory based words (or sub-modalities) you used to experience your emotions.

That's why we found four different words to describe your old phobia and reduced them down to just one. Not only did we find the core emotion; by describing your old fear using just one word we actually changed the memory or gestalt itself and practically one word is much easier to tackle than four.

listen to this therapy:
http://talkingcures.org/spider_phobia/audio

Okay, enough of the theory, now we are going to get practical and use this to de-program the emotional attachments you had around the old phobia. So to begin try this simple little exercise in how to reduce the emotions of a memory. This will take about 4-5 minutes, so start when you are ready.

Step One - Pick a Memory

For this first example I would like you to choose a happy memory. Perhaps choose a holiday; an achievement or a successful milestone or event in your life. Please don't pick something around a person, instead choose a walk on a beach, winning a promotion, something general and non-specific. Once you have a suitable happy memory go to step two.

Step Two - Score the emotional intensity of the memory

On a scale of one to ten (sound familiar?) one being low, no emotion and ten being high, ecstatic score how good this memory makes you feel. See what you saw, hear what you heard and feel what you felt and score the memory out of ten. Ideally you want to pick a memory that will score between 7 and 9. When you have a suitable memory you are ready to move on.

What we will do now is to change that memory by changing its visual representation. During the process just be aware of how each of the differences effect the memory. You will find that one of the changes, and I don't know which one it will be for you, will have the biggest effect. And don't worry any changes we make will be wiped away at the end of the exercise, so the memory will be back to good as and perhaps better than ever.

Step Three - Let's makes some changes

So you have a picture of this happy memory in your mind. Let me ask you a question about that picture:

Is the picture moving or still?

Go with the first answer that pops into your head, your first instinct. For most people high scoring memories have some degree of movement to them. So if that's the case and yours is moving make it a freeze-frame, stop it now, and turn it into a still picture. If it was already a still image then turn it upside down. Now leaving the picture of your memory exactly the way it is s freeze frame and upside down ask yourself, if you were to know;

Is the picture colour or black and white?

Again go with your first answer. If it's colour then make it black and white. If it's already black and white then turn the contrast way, way down so that it fades to murky grey. And finally leaving the image just like that, make it smaller. Smaller and smaller as small as a postage stamp at arms-length - tiny and distant. Make it really small and keep it at arms-length.

Step Four - Score the new memory again

Keeping the memory exactly where it is small, black and white and still at arms-length, how much emotional attachment does it have right now. Score it from one to ten. One being low, ten being high. Compare this score to your earlier score. Is the new score for that memory now lower than it was before? For 97% of people who have a highly developed visual sense then the answer will be yes. Now obviously I have no idea what score you started on or how far it went down, in a way that's not the important thing, what's important is that there was a downward direction and that you noticed the difference, as the emotion drained out of the previously happy memory.

Step Five – return the memory

Now make the memory just as it was before, if it was large make it large, if it was in colour make it colourful, if it was the right way up and moving then make it move again. Make it as happy, and emotionally charged as it was before we started. Once it is, you have completed the process. Over the next few interventions I'll be taking you through this style of exercise again specifically to remove the intensity of that old phobia. So that we can eradicate all of the emotions attached to that old phobia memory.

Some homework

Before moving to the next session, practice this technique. Choose another memory and repeat this exercise as it will help you to become more familiar with the process. In particular practice using this technique on any unwanted or unpleasant old memories and when you do stop at step four to leave the old unwanted memory with all of the emotion drained out of it. You'll be amazed how quick you become an expert at re-writing previous unpleasant experiences.

Chapter Seven: Removing any secondary gain

So far so good. Now let's begin to remove the hold that spiders had over you. In the last session we discovered exactly what core emotion was driving your fear of spiders. Now, as we move forward it's helpful to understand exactly why that core emotion had such a lasting hold over you. Earlier, I suggested that all phobias have common elements and that knowing these common elements makes the phobia easier to remove, or reduce to a point where it no longer bothers you, remember that?

Why this spider phobia had been with you for so long is another one of these common elements. It is the reason why up until now, this old fear of spiders has been so difficult to shake off. Although it might seem odd, as you go through this session you'll begin to appreciate exactly why something has been holding you back.

A common element with all phobias is something we call secondary gain. Essentially, despite all of the problems your spider problem has created for you in your life, all of the pain you have felt, all of the time you have spent worrying about the next time, despite all of this at some level, deep down a part of you believes that this fear has a benefit and that this fear keeps you safe.

To explain how this works we should talk a little about how we humans are programmed respond to things. All of us are hardwired to instinctively avoid pain and seek out pleasure. It's been well documented and researched, you may even have heard of Freud's Pain/Pleasure principle.

This avoid pain, seek pleasure response has been part of our survival instinct since the dawn of humanity. Many scientists believe that it's part of our evolutionary inheritance - and at its basic level an essential part of keeping us safe and well.

Let me give you an example of how this instinct works

Imagine that during that significant emotional event, the one that triggered your spider phobia, the event that we revisited in session one, you were actually caused pain or emotional distress. Before that event spiders didn't bother you at all because they had no emotional connection.

But when that event happened that all changed. That part of you that protects you from harm would have registered that:

spiders = pain

and because pain also = avoid

you naturally made the link that spiders = avoid.

And that important connection, that vital piece of survival information was tucked away in your memory, ready to surface whenever it felt you needed to avoid pain, which meant whenever you came into close contact with spiders. Not only that your in-build survival mechanism made sure that you would avoid spiders by giving you a way to recognise when you were in danger from spiders - the emotion you now feel whenever they surface in your life.

So, if you just thought about the phobia just in that context, as a way to avoid pain, then your natural survival instinct would have served its purpose and provided a valuable pain avoiding service. And that's the secondary gain - the benefit that the phobia provides, however small, insignificant or impractical it may be. Recognising that you have secondary gain is a really important step so let me say that last sentence again. Secondary gain is the benefit that your fear of spider provides, however small, insignificant, impractical or ridiculous it may seem.

At this point you might say to me, "that's all well and good but the secondary gain - whatever it may be for me - simply doesn't even begin to outweigh the problems that the phobia causes!" You are right of course, I'd have to agree with you. And if your phobia was a logical, rational decision you would be absolutely correct - and you could easily rationalise it away in a heartbeat.

But the truth is that phobia's don't work rationally, if they did you would have been rid of it ages ago, Phobias and fears work on a deeper emotional level, at the same level as your survival instinct, and to get rid of it we need to remove it at that level. That's why some of the interventions (phobia cures) that we are about to use will make no sense whatsoever, some may seem a bit strange, others downright odd. But that's the point, they are not meant to make sense - not to your rational mind anyway - but they will to your emotional mind and that's exactly where the changes need to be made.

Until you know what your secondary gain is it will be hard to reduce and remove the phobia. Essentially what this session does is to discover your secondary gain and help you find a way to keep it, or the essence of it, but without the phobic reaction to spiders. This is an important point because if we were to remove the secondary gain completely, which the interventions we are about to use will do, then your survival instinct would cut in and override them. Whilst it is possible we would have some short term success, chances are that they wouldn't last because that survival instinct would kick back in.

listen to this therapy:
http://talkingcures.org/spider_phobia/audio

Intervention for Secondary Gain

For a long lasting cure to your phobia we have to work with your secondary gain and find a way to satisfy it without the excessive phobic reaction. I'd recommend that you listen to the audio as it is as close as I can get to guiding you through this process. Now let's get around to finding your secondary gain.

Step One – What is the downside of your Phobia

Write down all of the negatives, problems and downsides that your phobia causes. Write down as much as you can, in as much detail as you can. When you are done review what you have written and pick one word top sum it all up. Pick just one word and write it down.

Now, stop for a minute. At this point it's important to change your state so stand up walk around, make yourself a drink, anything that will take your mind off step 1.

Step Two – What's the upside to your secondary gain?

Now pretend you are the part of you that controls secondary gain. Write down all of the benefits or positives that it causes or could cause - however insignificant. Again when you are done review what you have written and pick one word top sum it all up. Write it down.

Chances are that your first list will be much longer than your second list! Once more, stop for a moment and change your state. Get up, move, stretch do something different to change your state.

Step Three - Future changes

Imagine, for a moment, that I could just click my fingers and your old phobia had magically disappeared now. With a click of the fingers it was gone, the old fear that is. Imagine it now, I click my fingers and all of the fear of spiders is totally gone. Click.

Write down all of the things that have changed; how you feel, the things you can do differently, how much more control you now have, write down everything. Take some time to capture everything as this is the fun part.

Okay, one last time look at what you have just written and pick one word top sum it all up. Write it down.

Step Four - Intervention for changing your secondary gain

Then from the last session (session 3) you discovered your core emotion. Do you remember what it was? What is the opposite of that core emotion? So for example if it was 'Fear' then its opposite may be 'Joy'. Whatever your core emotion is, trust your instinct and take the first word that pops into your head for its opposite. Write in down, remember it and ask yourself the following questions:

This works best if you write out the questions below, inserting the appropriate words before asking yourself the questions;

"Is the [insert core emotion] I feel about spiders part of the secondary gain that keeps me safe?"

If yes continue. If no go back and repeat step two and add two other benefits. Go with the first thing that pops into your head.

"Would it be okay for me to continue to be safe from spiders and feel less [insert core emotion], experience less [insert

phobia downside] and have increased feelings like [insert future changes]?"

If yes continue. If no ask yourself:

"What else would I need to add to step three in order for it to be okay?"

Make a note of the answer that pops into your head and go back to repeat step two. Once that's done I'll share some quick interventions you can use to control your emotions 'in the moment'.

Chapter Eight: The emotion switch

In this session we will use a practical technique to change the feelings associated with that old spider phobia. At this point I feel I should make a small confession. I used to have a bit of an issue with spiders (notice the language I use to describe the experience). It was caused by an experience I had about 10 years ago. Like many people I keep a glass of water on my bedside cabinet at night. In the night I woke up and had a drink of water not realising before it was too late that a large, hairy spider had fallen into the glass. Luckily I didn't swallow it, because as soon as I felt this this alien squirming lump in my mouth I instinctively spat it out.

But although I didn't realise it at the time, the incident did change my reaction to spiders. The next time I saw a spider the feelings I felt on that night of surprise, repulsion and shock surfaced again. It should have been no surprise really as that's the way that significant emotional events condition our behaviour, emotions and reactions. I realised there and then that I needed to do a little work on myself to stop this developing into something else, to 'nip it in the bud' so to speak.

This was the technique I used to reset my emotions back to neutral. It worked just fine, that said ever since I have made sure that my glass is covered at night. I may have wiped away those feelings of anxiety but that doesn't mean that I want to repeat the experience.

Actually I use this technique a lot for other things as well, just before I do any public speaking or TV work or on the odd occasion I start to feel a headache or a cold coming on. In fact it's a great one-technique-fix for many, many things. It's ideal for changing your mood or state of mind and can be used for just about anything; it's one of those must-have techniques.

I know I have given it a big build up, so let me tell you exactly why, with a little bit of the theory, before we start to use it.

The reason this phobia treatment is so effective is because feelings and emotions have a structure, in the same way as memories have a structure. If you remember in the last session, we played around with the structure of your visual memory by changing some of its components. Changing the structure of the emotion begins to change the emotion itself. In the same way that when you start to remove some bricks from a wall, it undermines the structure, makes it weaker. If you keep removing bricks eventually the wall will become so weak, so unstable that it will simply collapse under its own weight.

The principle here is very similar, we are going to change the way that you feel about those old emotions that surround your fear of spiders. By changing them bit by bit we will undermine their structure, make them weaker so that they change and collapse.

There is a difference between this intervention and the other sessions we have had in the past. Because this is a feelings based intervention it involves movement, so it is best if you stand up. Yes, I did say stand up and let me guide you through the process.

So are you standing comfortably? Then we'll begin. If you feel you'll get more out of this session if you let me guide you through this session, as before you can listen to the intervention.

listen to this therapy:
http://talkingcures.org/spider_phobia/audio

Step One - Remember the last time you had your fear of spiders

Take a moment to think back to that time. Then remembering what you can see what you saw, hear what you heard, think what you thought and most importantly feel what you were feeling. When you start to feel those emotions become intense then score them using the SUDS scale.

Step Two - Score the emotions

On a scale of one to ten one being low, no emotion not bothered at all and ten being high, anxiety, fear and dread, score how that last experience felt. Score the experience out of ten.

Score 1-2-3-4-5-6-7-8-9-10

If you have scored the emotion anything above a three then you will have felt that it has an emotional energy. As all energy has a flow, a movement I want you to get a sense of how this energy moves. In a moment I'm going to ask you to use your right hand to trace the movement of the emotion you feel.

To get a sense of how this emotion 'moves' there are basically two types of movement that make the difference; direction and frequency. The direction can be up and down, left and right or backwards and forwards. Frequency can be short fast movements or long slow movements.

Now, we'll describe the emotion in those terms

So use your right hand and begin to move it either up and down, left or right or in and out.

Do it now. Go with your gut feel and choose the movement that feels right for the emotion. If you are not sure try them all and settle on the one movement that best connects with the feeling.

Ok with your right hand moving either in and out or left and right or up and down adjust the speed or frequency of the movement. Fears and phobias tend to have a frequency that is shorter and faster so adjust the tempo to suit the emotion.

Once you have connected with the movement of the emotion and you have the direction and the frequency of the emotion then you are ready to start making some changes.

Step Three - Changing the feeling

First we will change the frequency of the emotion, so start to slow your hand movement down and at the same time, make the distance your hand travels further, perhaps two, three or four times as long. Begin slowing the movement down and making the stroke longer and longer.

Keeping the frequency as it is, now change the direction, so if you hands was moving up and down switch to left and right. If the movement is in and out then change to up and down. Or if left and right move change to in and out. The important thing is to change both the frequency and direction. And as you do notice that the emotion also changes. It changes because you have changed its structure to something more relaxed and comfortable.

Continue this relaxed and comfortable hand movement and remember back to the last time you had your fear of spiders. Keep your hand moving in that relaxed and comfortable way and take a moment to think back to that time, see what you saw, hear what you heard, think what you thought and most importantly feel what you were feeling.

Then score this new feeling using the SUDS scale.

Score 1-2-3-4-5-6-7-8-9-10

Step four - Score the new experience

Keeping your hand moving in this relaxed and comfortable way, score how you feel. Score the feelings from one to ten. One being low no emotion, ten being high.

Ok you can stop moving your hand now.

Compare this new score to your earlier score. Is the new score lower than it was before? Then well done, you have learnt a valuable strategy to reduce the emotion you used to feel around spiders. And the best part is that, after you have practiced this technique a few times you can use this process the next time you need to remain calm and relaxed.

To do this, simply run through the process again just before and if necessary during the time you need to remain calm.

That's what I do, especially if I'm having some serious dental work. The only thing I do differently is that instead of standing up and moving my hand around in an exaggerated way - which might look a bit odd, even for me - I run through the process in my head and make small, little, micro hand movements. The type of small hand movements that no one would ever notice. The calming effect is just the same it reduces any anxiety or nervousness to something that is more relaxed and comfortable.

Your homework

Next time you are confronted by an event that makes you feel those old feelings just start to move your hand in that relaxed and comfortable way and notice how the emotion drains out of the situation.

Or you could put yourself in a situation which had it happened previously would have made you feel uncomfortable and now be aware of how you feel differently.

Chapter Nine: The music therapy

This music therapy is one of my more effective spider phobia cures. I feel you'll like it too. Now, do you recall a few sessions ago I talked about how we represent our memories using our five senses of touch, vision, sound, taste and smell?

Well in this therapy we are going to use one of them to help us reduce any negative emotions that you may still have surrounding spiders.

You might be a little surprised to learn that of all the senses we could use, the one that we will be using is sound. There is a very good reason for this; sound is especially powerful at evoking memories that have strong emotions. You will have already experienced how this works; in fact you could well experience it every day without realising it.

Firstly, let me ask you a question. Is there any music that when you hear it, it reminds you of an event, a memory, a significant time in your past? Of course there is, it is a universal experience, everyone has music that reminds them of specific events, times and people in their lives. These pieces of music act as triggers for significant times in our lives. Although we all have these triggers, the difference is that we have our own music 'the soundtrack of our lives' that triggers those memories.

We have all had the experience of hearing a piece of music and being transported back to a significant time in our lives. That's why this music therapy so effective. So, as long as you have been reminded of a memory from your past because of a piece of music, then this therapy will work well for you.

The way that this music therapy works is that we are going to associate a piece of music with your earliest memory of being scared of spiders. So that we have the greatest chance of making a big difference, I'm going to select the piece of music we will use. I've chosen it because it is the exact opposite of how you would have felt at the time. It's a funny, crazy, silly piece of music. By playing it while thinking of the memory will effectively change the way you feel about spiders.

Music provides an effective cure for spider phobias

The way this music therapy works is that by playing the music and reliving that original spider fear at the same time, both become confused. This confusion has the effect of stripping out any emotion associated with your experience of spiders. Effectively your old memories of spiders will have the emotion taken away and these memories will replace the original memories and the fear will simply fade away.

This music therapy works so well that you may even find, to your surprise, that the next time you find yourself in a stressful situation or come into contact with a spider, this piece of music just pops into your head - making all of the negative emotion drain away. You may even find that you laugh out loud at the thought - and I guess you haven't done that around spiders for a while!

So my goal for this session is that you find that the emotional intensity of that old phobia dramatically reduces during this session and whenever the piece of music pops into your head. Does that sound good? If so let's get started.

As before my preference would be that you let me talk you through the session, simply because it allows you to concentrate on the music therapy, rather than having to read and listen at the same time. You'll probably need around eight to ten minutes to do this session, so find somewhere nice and quiet where you can listen without being disturbed.

listen to this therapy:
http://talkingcures.org/spider_phobia/audio

Remember that first time you had your fear of spiders

Remember that old memory, that first time you felt that old fear of spiders. Take a moment to think back to that time, see what you saw, hear what you heard, think what you thought and feel what you were feeling. When those feelings become intense then score them using the subjective units of distress scale.

Score how you feel, on the SUD scale of 1 to 10.

Score 1-2-3-4-5-6-7-8-9-10

On a scale of one to ten one being low, no emotion not bothered at all and ten being high, anxiety, fear and dread, score how that first experience felt. Score the memory out of ten and make a note of the score.

Play the music

If you are reading this and not listening to the audio therapy play, the music download, play it as loud as you can and remembering that first experience, try to hold onto those old feelings.

You may find it difficult but try to feel those feelings that you used to feel when thinking about spiders. Do your best to remember that first time, feeling what you felt, seeing what you saw, hearing what you heard and thinking what you thought. Don't let the music disturb you too much as you try to remember again that very first time you were bothered by spiders.

Score how you feel now on the SUD scale of 1 to 10.

Score 1-2-3-4-5-6-7-8-9-10

Keep the music playing and load and try not to laugh out loud, score how you feel right now. Score the new feelings from that first experience from one to ten. One being low no emotion, ten being high.

Compare this new score to your earlier score

Is the new score lower than your first score? Then well done, you have learnt another useful strategy to reduce the emotion you used to feel around spiders. And the best part is that, whenever you now think about spiders this piece of music will just pop into your head and you will feel more relaxed and comfortable. You may even have to suppress the urge to smile or laugh out loud.

Future testing

With the music still playing (if it's stopped then please start it again) think of a time in the future, which had it happened in the past, would have made you feel those feelings of anxiety around spiders. Think of a specific time, a particular situation with the music playing. Now notice how differently you feel right with the music playing.

Be aware of how it is making you feel differently, now enjoy that new feeling, safe in the knowledge that whenever that music pops into your head you will feel more relaxed around spiders. And, the funny thing is that whenever you are around spiders that music will just pop into your head.

Being more relaxed is a great way to feel, isn't it?

Chapter Ten: Word replacement therapy

This little known spider phobia intervention will reduce any fear of spiders. So we are three interventions into the spider phobia cure and I hope that you are beginning to notice the effect they are having. During a journey like this one, it is often a good idea to stop and review how far we have travelled, reflect on what has gone before and take a time out. Take time to review the milestones along the way, look back on the distance you have travelled.

Often in our lives we achieve great things, but don't give ourselves credit for them because we don't give ourselves a frame of reference that helps us to realise just how far we have come. It's true that I'm English and we are notoriously good at hiding our successes and focussing on our shortcomings but I feel it's something we all do from time to time. That's why it is useful to stop. And reflect on the journey so far. Only then when we look back on the progress we have made, take note of our progress and be ready for the journey to come.

Now, three interventions in, we have reached that point in our journey together. It is time to reflect on the progress you have made in removing your old phobia of spiders. The best way to do that is to take you back to session two. If you can remember back that far you described how that old fear of spiders made you feel. I asked you to recall those old feelings and write down four words that summed up the experience back then.

We won't be using the subjective units of distress scale for this exercise. Although SUDS is perfect for measuring the effect of a treatment, I want to share a treatment with you that can be used to change how you feel about anything that troubles you.

And I do mean anything - including a fear of spiders. When I first found this technique it was being used as a way to control pain. I was sceptical at first because it seemed so simple but I was eager to try it out for myself.

How this Phobia Cure Works

This easy to use technique works on the principle that the words we use to describe our experience are much more than a simple description. They actually help define and determine the experience itself. The words you use as much as the event itself will determine how you remember the experience. They determine the intensity of the feelings, thoughts and sensations that surround the experience and most importantly how you experience it right now.

Let me give you an example: If you have a bad day and choose describe the experience as a "total bloody disaster" the day will, irrespective of what actually happened, feel much worse that if you had chosen to describe it as "a tad inconvenient". Research on this technique suggests that the words you use actually stimulate different neurological pathways in the brain. And it is these different pathways that define the experience. Now to be honest I don't know if that is exactly how it works but I do know that it does, so either way something is happening.

So about a month after I found this technique, an opportunity presented itself to put this theory into practice. I had at that time taken on a client who was suffering from chronic backache. It was so bad that she was, at that time, incapacitated and was bedridden. Like many clients she came to me out of desperation, a last resort as she had tried all modern (western) forms of pain control. These had worked for a while but as time progressed each pain control drug had become less and less effective. As her pain increased her medical practitioner had switched her to another drug but her problem was that, by the time I was involved, she had exhausted all the prescription drugs available.

Initially I would have used hypnosis with this client because it works very well for pain control. The downside of hypnosis is that there are many preconceptions surrounding it and it can take a number of sessions to help the client to a point where they can control this type of relentless pain. So in this instance I decided to use the technique I'm about to guide you through.

The result surprised even me. Remember that this was the first time I had worked with her and this intervention took less than five minutes to complete. In that time her pain level went from a SUDS 9 out of 10 which was excruciating, debilitating, unbearable and incessant to a SUDS 3 out of 10 which was uncomfortable, irritating, inconvenient and a nuisance.

Not only did my client's score go from a 9 to a 3, her experience of the pain and how it affected her changed so much that from being bedridden just five minutes before the treatment afterwards she could get up and walk around with little or no discomfort. This was something she hadn't been able to do for over a week and she felt no excruciating or debilitating pain.

Despite my calm and reserved bedside manner, inside I was amazed that a techniques that was so simple could have such an immediate and profound effect. After my visit, my client used this method of pain control so effectively that I never saw her again! Although we keep in touch - in fact we still talk about once a month - to date she hasn't needed to resort to drugs to manage her back pain.

The other great benefit of this intervention is that once you know how to use it, you can use it for all sorts of problems both physiological and psychological.

The Word Replacement Intervention

The best attitude to have towards this therapy is to treat is as a game. So put any conscious thoughts, any logic to one side and just play along. Like any game this one has rules to play by. For this game you'll need those original four words. Those words that were written down in the 'secondary gain' session, the four words you originally used back then to describe your fear of spiders. Ideally, if you have the original piece of paper you wrote then down on that will be perfect. If not write them down so you have them in front of you on a piece of paper. Only continue when you have them in front of you.

Now here are the rules of the game.

Rule 1. Whenever a word that is written down on the piece of paper is crossed out then that word is removed from your vocabulary. It ceases to exist, it's gone forever, it is erased from your memory.

Rule 2. Because any word that has been crossed out has gone forever, obviously it can't be used again.

That's it there are no more rules to the game. I told you it was an easy game to play!

Now there are just five steps to you need to follow to play this game.

Step 1. In turn cross out each word. By that I mean scribble it out, obliterate it, so that you cannot recognise it anymore.

Step 2. Replace the word you just obliterated with a new word.

Step 3. Repeat steps 1 and 2 so that each of the original four words is obliterated and replaced with four new words.

Step 4. Repeat steps 1 and 2 so that each of the new words used in step 3 is obliterated and replaced with new words.

Step 5. Write down the following sentence "The words I use to describe how I feel about spiders are, 1st step 4 word, 2nd step 4 word, 3rd step 4 word and 4th step four word."

Play our little game and you might also be aware that by changing the words that you use to describe your experience, the way you feel about spiders also changes. If you would like me to talk you through the process then play the audio therapy. If not then just play by the rules and complete steps 1 to 5.

Once you have done that I'd like you to think about a time in the future when you would be in a situation that involves spiders. Take a little time to think of that situation and see what you would see, hear what you would hear, think what you would think and feel what you would feel.

Sum up all of these sensations with your four new words that describe that experience. Look at your four new words as you think about that situation that involves spiders and notice how you also feel differently now.

Remember that during a journey like this one, it is often a good idea to stop and review how far we have travelled, reflect on what has gone before and take a time out. And if you review the milestones along the way, look back on the distance you have travelled, you will have noticed that spiders were just part of that journey and are now firmly behind you.

Chapter Eleven: Disconnect the connection

Do you remember that earlier we talked about how to before you can successfully break the association between the phobia and the emotions it triggers you should realise that, at an unconscious level, the purpose of this connection 'or phobia' was to protect you from emotional pain? So to successfully remove the phobia your unconscious mind needs to know you are safe. That's why it is important to use the 'Time to Change' script before using any of these interventions. So just to check ask yourself the following questions.

"Is it ok to continue to be totally safe and finally remove all remaining negative emotions associated with the phobia?"

"Would it be ok to experience the emotion surrounding the phobia reducing, whilst remaining totally safe?"

Continue if you get a quick and decisive "YES". Otherwise go back to the 'it's time to change script" for a quick refresh.

This intervention is specifically designed to break the link and remove the emotional attachment of the phobia. This process is most effective when used quickly and should be repeated until the old emotion is gone or reduced to an insignificant level. You'll need a mobile phone, some imagination and a little peace and quiet for this intervention. Here's the thing about imagination, or visualising something, some people actually see an images, some feel it's happening, some get a sense of it, others go through the motions trusting in the process. All of these are perfectly fine. However you use your imagination will work for this intervention.

listen to this therapy:
http://talkingcures.org/spider_phobia/audio

Step One. Calibrate the intensity of the feeling. If you have to think about it, the phobia on a scale of 1 (low emotion, relaxed, not bothered) to 10 (scared, physical reaction, terrified), how would you feel right now. Go with the first number that pops into your head.

Score 1-2-3-4-5-6-7-8-9-10

Step Two. You'll need either a mobile phone with a screen or a TV or computer monitor with a small (less than 12") screen. Find a quiet place to relax.

Step Three. Place the mobile at least three feet away (eight feet if you are using a TV or computer monitor) and above your eye line. Keep it turned off.

Step Four. Imagine that you are watching that old phobia play out in black and white, on the screen and watch yourself in the movie. When the movie ends imagine it playing backwards, at double speed in colour. If the images are to emotive simply move further away from the screen until you feel sufficiently relaxed to continue.

Step Five. Repeat this process, watching the movie forwards in black and white and backwards in colour at least four more times, each time letting the process get faster and faster.

Step Six. When you are done, picture the screen turning off, with the central white dot disappearing into the distance. Stretch and take a few deep breaths before you continue.

Step Seven. Now imagine a situation in the future, which had it happened before, would have caused you to feel those old phobic emotions. Notice how it feels different now, and that the feelings associated with it have changed, perhaps even dissolved away.

Step Eight. Now take hold of the mobile phone and with those changes and differences in mind score on a scale of 1-10 how you feel now?

Score 1-2-3-4-5-6-7-8-9-10

Squeeze the phone in your hand.

However much your score as reduced, take that as a sign that you now have the means to control these emotions. Should you need to repeat this intervention you will find that the intensity of the emotion attached to the phobia continues to reduce until it totally disappears. What you are experiencing is the link being dissolved at an unconscious level, continue until it disappears totally or is reduced to an insignificant level.

Some homework

If you are ever in a situation that would have in the past triggered those old feelings simply hold your phone and gently squeeze it. You'll find that this will make those feelings simply fade away.

Chapter Twelve: And finally

How would you like an intervention that makes you smile and feel good instantly? This will boost your self-esteem as the opinion we have of ourselves, our self-esteem, develops and evolves during our lives. Our self-esteem evolves constantly through our experiences with different people and situations, but the basic patterns and trends are created early in our lives. Our experiences during childhood play a major role in the shaping of our basic self-esteem. So influential are the first seven years of our lives that they are often referred to in psychology as the 'imprint period'. During this time the reaction to our successes and failures by our immediate family and friends all contribute to the creation of our basic self-esteem.

Experiences and opinions formed during the imprint period act as a filter for later information. The filter effectively blocks any information that doesn't fit our existing self-esteem model. People with low self-esteem are more likely to filter out any positive information and readily accept negative information. The more negative information they accept, the lower their self-esteem.

We have all witnessed the effect of these filters. Have you ever paid someone a compliment only for that person to not hear it, not believe it or dismiss it? Have you ever been paid a compliment and ignored it, rejected it or been suspicious of the person's motives? If so, that is the filtering process at work.

Many research projects have identified the effects of these filters. Having reviewed many such projects, Stephane Dandeneau PhD and Prof. Mark Baldwin of McGill University, Canada wrote in the Journal of Social and Clinical Psychology, "After a failure … individuals with low self-esteem tend to focus on the negative outcome, blame themselves for it, and draw uncharitable inferences about their abilities. Conversely, high self-esteem individuals engage in a variety of defensive processes. They engage in processing that is biased toward overestimation of their control over circumstances, overestimation of their performances, and a tendency to respond to any negative outcomes with external attributions and increased attention to alternative domains of strength…Therefore it seems that individuals with low self-esteem …have difficulty disengaging attention from, any minimal indication of negative interpersonal feedback."

Although many of the filters that create these behaviours are formed during our 'imprint period' they are not set in stone. Let me say that again they are not set in stone – they can change as easily as you have changed your old problem. They naturally change and evolve with the individual. However, if a person has low self-esteem then it's usually a sign that one or more of the filters has stuck in the past.

This intervention will change or bypass those old filters, the ones that cause you to choose to feel low. It is designed to break the cycle of negative interpersonal feedback. This therapy is really very, very powerful at making long term change. It is also quick to use, sometimes taking less than a minute from start to finish. Used on a regular basis it has positive long-term effect on your self-esteem. So don't be fooled by its apparent simplicity.

I feel good – I knew that I would!

Depending on how stuck your existing filters were you might need a little extra help to bypass them. The first time you use this intervention follow the four step process below. Not only will you feel better, it will give you an immediate, measurable and positive change to your self-esteem. Although in the future you'll be able to use the therapy almost anywhere, initially it is best conducted somewhere quiet, where you will not be disturbed. A comfortable room that has a mirror on the wall would be ideal.

Step One. To start, score on a scale of 1 (low self-esteem, negative, inadequate) to 10 (high self-esteem, confident, positive), how you feel right now. Trust your instinct and go with the first number that you feel is right.

Score 1-2-3-4-5-6-7-8-9-10

Step Two. Perform all of the actions in sequence from 1 through to 12. It is possible that you will be aware of how each of the actions changes the way you feel. That's because some will be more effective for you than others. You may even notice that many of the actions bring a smile to your face.

The twelve sure-fire ways to self-esteem action list

1. Remember a pleasant event or something you did that made you feel proud.

2. Give yourself a 15 second round of applause

3. Imagine something enjoyable that could happen today

4. Pat yourself on the back at least four times

5. Say "I like (the first thing that comes into your head)"

6. Look at your reflection and smile

7. Hum the first few bars of a favourite tune

8. Shake hands with yourself

9. Say or think "I'm good at (the first thing that comes into your head)"

10. Look at your reflection and wave

11. Draw three smiley faces – if no paper is available try doing it with your eyes!

12. Say or think "I enjoy (the first thing that comes into your head)"

Step Three. How better do you feel? Score how you feel right now on a scale of 1 (low self-esteem, negative, inadequate) to 10 (high self-esteem, confident, positive), how you feel right now. Go with the first number you feel is right.

Score 1-2-3-4-5-6-7-8-9-10

Compare this with your old score. The difference between the scores shows the immediate effect of the esteem actions.

Step Four: To see a consistent improvement consider using this intervention every day for at least a week. If you find that there are one or two of the actions that make you feel good then just use them. Either way use it on a regular basis.

From now on, this intervention takes the form of a game. It is similar to that old children's favourite 'Simon says'. Play the game to raise your self-esteem and feel better about yourself. Like 'Simon says' you are directed to follow the instructions and undertake a series of simple, random, positive actions. Unlike 'Simon says', all of these actions are designed to bypass your existing filters and start to break down any existing cycle of negative reinforcement. Play the game on a regular basis – at least once a day for the first week – and you will soon notice a lasting difference.

The rules of the game are simple.

Rule One. Close your eyes. Randomly place your index finger on the number grid below.

Rule Two. Find the corresponding number on the Actions List.

Rule Three. Complete the action, suggestion or task.

Rule Four. Repeat rule one and keep a running total of the numbers chosen.

Rule Five. Continue playing until you reach either a total score in excess of 24 or have repeated the process a minimum of seven times.

The 24/7 Self-Esteem Number Grid.

People, who regularly play the game, soon notice a shift in behaviour. Apart from feeling better they become aware their old filters have changed when; they catch sight of their reflection and smile; or hear themselves humming their favourite songs; or perhaps realise they have been doodling and have drawn smiley faces.

I wonder how you will notice that things have changed?

However you notice them, these changes in behaviour take them as a sign that the old filters have been permanently bypassed and replaced with something new.

And that thing will be more control over your feelings, emotions and behaviours.

--0—

Now you have all of the tools you need to make that old thing with spiders disappear. Practice these techniques and more importantly choose the one or two that worked best for you and use them. The more you use them, the more of a habit they will become. The more something is a habit the more you will instinctively use it in the future should you ever need to.

Printed in Poland
by Amazon Fulfillment
Poland Sp. z o.o., Wrocław